Dresden Fan
Quilts and Coordinating Projects for Your Home

CAROLANN M. PALMER

Martingale™
& COMPANY

Dresden Fan: Quilts and
Coordinating Projects for Your Home
© 2002 by Carolann M. Palmer

That Patchwork Place® is an imprint of
Martingale & Company™.

Martingale & Company
20205 144th Avenue NE
Woodinville, WA 98072-8478 USA
www.martingale-pub.com

Printed in China
07 06 05 04 03 02   8 7 6 5 4 3 2 1

CREDITS

President . . . . Nancy J. Martin
CEO . . . . Daniel J. Martin
Publisher . . . . Jane Hamada
Editorial Director . . . . Mary V. Green
Managing Editor . . . . Tina Cook
Technical Editors . . . . Dawn Anderson,
                                            Laurie Baker
Copy Editor . . . . Liz McGehee
Design Director . . . . Stan Green
Illustrator . . . . Robin Strobel
Cover and Text Designer . . . . Stan Green
Photographer . . . . Brent Kane

**Library of Congress Cataloging-in-Publication
data available upon request.**

ISBN 1-56477-435-X

MISSION STATEMENT

We are dedicated to providing quality products
and service by working together to inspire
creativity and to enrich the lives we touch.

Contents

Introduction

This book is based on a block I call the Dresden Fan Sampler block. The inspiration for this design came from the border of a kitchen towel. I asked myself, could this spiky-looking flower design become a Double Fan on a quilt border? Could this same Double Fan be used to frame a pieced sampler block? Then, I pulled out my graph paper and went to work, coming up with the basic block and border designs for the Dresden Fan Garden quilt (page 27). For each sampler block within the larger block design, I used patterns from Nancy J. Martin's *365 Quilt Blocks a Year Perpetual Calendar*.

After drawing the designs, I began the search for eight different gradated fabrics to match a favorite floral print. It took a while. (This was some time ago, and I could probably make several quilts from the rejects!) It is easier today to find a range of eight gradated fabrics because of the abundance of mottled and hand-dyed gradations that are now so popular. When you choose to make this quilt, be persistent in completing it! There is a lot of nice handwork in making the Double Fan and Dresden Fan designs, and also a lot of fun in making the sampler blocks. I must admit there was a time near the completion of the quilt when its name changed to "That Purple Thing," but persistence paid off and it is the most beautiful quilt I've ever made.

If you choose to make this quilt for a bed, you'll want to have some matching accessories to go with it. This book includes instructions for matching European square-pillow shams, ruffle-edged pillowcases, a dust ruffle, and a round toss pillow that features a complete Dresden Plate design in the center. If you want to try a smaller project before attempting the bed quilt, try making the wall hanging or table runner, also included in this book.

Rotary Cutting

The projects in this book include instructions for quick and easy rotary cutting wherever possible. All measurements include standard ¼"-wide seam allowances. For those unfamiliar with rotary cutting, a brief introduction is provided below.

1. Fold the fabric and match selvages, aligning the crosswise and lengthwise grains as much as possible. Place the folded edge closest to you on the cutting mat. Align a square ruler along the folded edge of the fabric; then place a long, straight ruler to the left of the square ruler, just covering the uneven raw edges on the left side of the fabric. Remove the square ruler and cut along the right edge of the long ruler, rolling the rotary cutter away from you. Discard this strip. (Reverse this procedure if you are left-handed.)

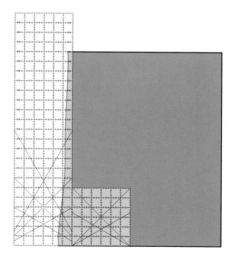

2. To cut strips, align the required measurements on the ruler with the newly cut edge of the fabric. For example, to cut a 2½"-wide strip, place the 2½" ruler mark on the edge of the fabric.

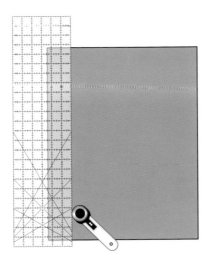

3. Turn the strips horizontally. Trim away the selvage ends of the strips. Align the required measurement on the ruler with the left edge of a strip and cut the desired shape and size.

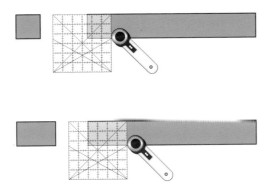

HALF-SQUARE TRIANGLES

Make half-square triangles by cutting a square in half on the diagonal. The triangle's short sides are on the straight grain of fabric.

1. Cut squares to the size indicated in the project instructions.

2. Stack squares and cut once diagonally, corner to corner. Each square yields two triangles.

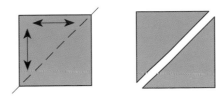

QUARTER-SQUARE TRIANGLES

Make quarter-square triangles by cutting a square in quarters on the diagonal. The triangle's long side is on the straight grain of fabric.

1. Cut squares to the size indicated in the project instructions.

2. Stack squares and cut twice diagonally, from corner to corner. Each square yields four triangles.

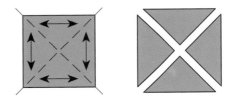

Freezer-Paper Appliqué

This method of appliqué uses freezer paper to stabilize the appliqué pieces during the appliqué process. The edge of the freezer paper is used as a guide for shaping the appliqué pieces and is especially helpful for producing smooth curves in the Dresden designs.

To make appliqué templates, use clear plastic. Plastic templates are more durable and more accurate than templates made from cardboard. Since you can see through the plastic, it's easy to trace the templates accurately.

Place template plastic over each pattern piece and trace with a fine-line permanent marker. Do not add seam allowances. Cut out the templates on the drawn lines. Mark the pattern name and grain-line arrow (if applicable) on the template.

1. Using a plastic template, trace the appliqué shape onto the dull (unwaxed) side of the freezer paper. If you are making several appliqué pieces with the same template shape, such as for the fan blades of the Dresden Plate, Double Fan, or Dresden Fan, stack several layers of freezer paper together and secure with a couple of staples through the center of the traced design. Cut on the marked lines and remove the staples to yield several freezer-paper templates of the same shape.

2. With a dry iron, fuse the freezer-paper templates, shiny side down, to the wrong side of the fabric. Allow at least ¾" between the templates.

3. Cut out the shapes ¼" from the edges of the freezer-paper templates, using a rotary cutter and ruler for the straight edges. Use scissors to trim around curves.

4. Stitch the pieces together and baste around the curved edges as instructed in "Piecing the Dresden Units" on page 7.

5. Position the appliqué unit on the background fabric and stitch in place, using the traditional appliqué stitch outlined on page 7. Cut away the background fabric behind the appliqué, ¼" from the stitching, as necessary, to remove the freezer-paper template. Be careful not to cut through the appliqué piece. Use a spray mister to spray lightly with water to loosen the bond if needed. Press.

Traditional Appliqué Stitch

The traditional appliqué stitch, or blind stitch, is appropriate for sewing all appliqué shapes, including sharp points and curves.

1. Tie a knot in a single strand of thread approximately 18" long.

2. Hide the knot by slipping the needle into the seam allowance from the wrong side of the appliqué piece, bringing the needle out on the fold line.

3. Work from right to left if you are right-handed, or left to right if you are left-handed. Start the first stitch by moving the needle straight off the appliqué, inserting the needle into the background fabric. Let the needle travel under the background fabric, parallel to the edge of the appliqué, bringing the needle up about ⅛" away along the pattern line.

4. As you bring the needle up, pierce the edge of the appliqué piece, catching only one or two threads of the folded edge.

5. Move the needle straight off the appliqué into the background fabric. Let your needle travel under the background, bringing it up about ⅛" away, again catching the edge of the appliqué.

6. Give the thread a slight tug and then continue stitching.

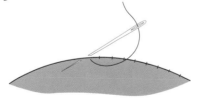

7. To end your stitching, pull the needle through to the wrong side. Take two small stitches behind the appliqué piece, making knots by taking your needle through the loops. Check the right side to see if the thread "shadows"

through your background. If it does, take one more small stitch on the back side to direct the tail of the thread under the appliqué fabric.

Piecing the Dresden Units

The quilt and several of the accessory projects are accented by appliquéd units made up of fan blades stitched together (template 3 on page 31). The number of blades in the appliqué determine the type of unit.

The Dresden Plate unit is made up of sixteen fan blades that are joined to make a circle; a circle of fabric covers the ends of the blades where they meet in the middle.

Dresden Plate

The Double Fan unit is made up of eight fan blades; a half-circle covers the ends of the blades.

Double Fan

The Dresden Fan is one-quarter of the Dresden Plate. It is made up of four fan blades with a quarter-circle covering the blade ends.

Dresden Fan

To make each type of unit:

1. Refer to "Freezer-Paper Appliqué" on page 5 to cut out the fan blade and circle, half-circle, or quarter-circle templates indicated in the project instructions from freezer paper, and fuse them to the appropriate fabrics. Cut out the shapes.

2. Stitch the blades needed for each unit together along the long edges; begin stitching at the narrow end, at the edge of the fabric, and stop ¼" from the curved edge. Press the seam allowances open. Make the number of units required by the project directions.

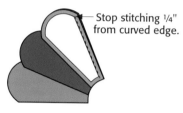

Stop stitching ¼" from curved edge.

3. On the curved edges of the fan blades and the circle, half-circle, and/or quarter-circle pieces, hand baste ⅛" from the raw edges, pulling up the thread to gather the fabric around the template. Secure with a couple of stitches through all layers. Press.

4. Referring to "Traditional Appliqué Stitch" on page 7, appliqué the unit to the base fabric as indicated in the project instructions.

5. Appliqué the circle, half-circle, or quarter-circle over the raw ends of the fan blades. For the Dresden Plate unit, place the circle so that it covers the raw edges where the narrow ends meet. For the Double Fan unit, align the straight edges of the half-circle with the background piece and cover the raw edges of the blades. For the Dresden Fan unit, align the straight edges of the quarter-circle with the straight edges of the background square.

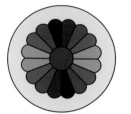

Dresden Plate

Double Fan

Dresden Fan

6. Refer to "Freezer-Paper Appliqué" on page 5 to cut away the background fabric and remove the freezer-paper templates.

Covered Cording

Covered cording inserted into seams or used as edging on pillows gives your projects a professional look. Ready-made covered cording is available from fabric shops, but to get the perfect color match, you may wish to make your own. Determine the amount of covered cording needed by measuring the length of the area to be edged, then add 10" to 15" extra for seams and finishing. Purchase the determined amount of uncovered $\frac{3}{16}$"-diameter cotton cord and follow the instructions on page 9 to cover it.

To cover ³⁄₁₆"-diameter cord:

1. Align the 45° line on your ruler with the straight edge of your fabric and cut 1½"-wide bias strips.

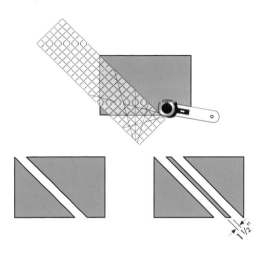

2. Sew the bias strips, right sides together, at right angles, allowing for ½" seam allowances. Press the seam allowances open.

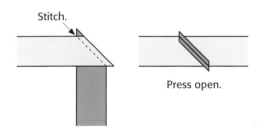

3. Wrap the bias strip around the cord with wrong sides together and raw edges even. Stitch along the edge of the cord, using a zipper foot.

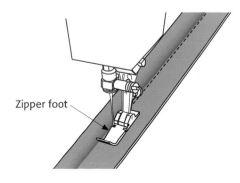

To attach covered cording:

1. Pin the cording, right sides together, to the edge of the fabric piece to be trimmed, starting at least 4" away from any corners.

2. Pin the cording all the way around. Trim the excess, allowing a 1" overlap. Rip out the stitching on one end of the cording for about 2". Pull the end of the cotton cording out of the casing. Trim the excess cording so that the ends just meet. Turn under ³⁄₈" on the end of the bias strip, and insert the remaining end into the strip. Fold the bias strip back around the cording, and pin in place.

3. Stitch the covered cording to the edge of the fabric, using a zipper foot or cording foot. Clip curves if necessary. Remove pins as you come to them.

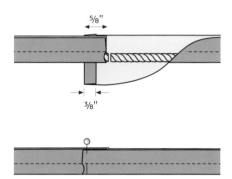

4. Position the corded fabric piece and second fabric piece, right sides together, with the corded piece on top. Sew the pieces together, stitching on the previous stitching line or slightly inside it to prevent the previous stitching from showing in the finished project.

Binding

For a French double-fold binding, cut 2½"-wide strips across the width of the fabric. You'll need enough strips to go around the perimeter of the quilt, plus 10" for seams and mitered corners.

1. Sew strips, right sides together, to make one long piece of binding. Join the strips at right angles and stitch across the corner as shown. Trim excess fabric and press the seams open.

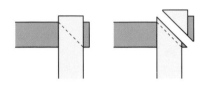

2. Fold the strip in half lengthwise, wrong sides together, and press. Cut one end at a 45° angle; press the cut end under ¼".

Fold line

3. Trim the batting and backing even with the quilt top. For a firmer binding, trim the batting and backing ¼" from the quilt top edge.

4. Starting on one side of the quilt and using a ¼"-wide seam allowance, stitch the binding to the quilt, keeping the raw edges even with the quilt-top edge. End the stitching ¼" from the corner of the quilt and backstitch. Clip the thread.

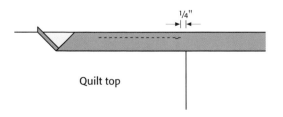

¼"

Quilt top

5. Turn the quilt so that you'll be stitching down the next side. Fold the binding up, away from the quilt, then back down onto itself, parallel with the edge of the quilt top. Begin stitching at the edge, backstitching to secure. Repeat on the remaining edges and corners of the quilt.

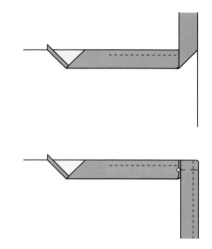

6. When you reach the beginning of the binding, stop stitching. Overlap the starting edge of the binding by about 1" and cut away any excess binding, trimming the end at a 45° angle. Tuck the end of the binding into the fold and finish the seam.

7. Fold the binding over the raw edges of the quilt to the back, with the folded edge covering the row of machine stitching, and blindstitch in place. A miter will form at each corner. Blindstitch the mitered corners.

Quilt back

Sampler Blocks

All of the blocks in this section finish to 12". When making the projects in this book, feel free to substitute a 12" block of your choice for the one used in the project. The key below shows the different fabrics featured in the sampler blocks. Note that not all of the fabrics appear in each block.

Fabric Key

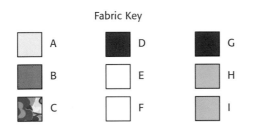

After stitching your quilt blocks together, take the time to square them up. Use a large square ruler to measure your blocks and make sure they are the desired size, plus an extra ¼" on each edge for seam allowances. For example, if you are making 12" blocks, they should all measure 12½" before you sew them together. If your blocks vary slightly in size, trim the larger blocks to match the size of the smallest one. Be sure to trim all four sides; otherwise, your block will be lopsided. If your blocks are not the required finished size, you'll have to adjust all the other components of the quilt accordingly.

FLYING SHUTTLES

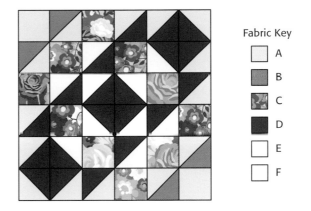

Fabric Key

A
B
C
D
E
F

Fabric	First Cut	Second Cut
A	7 squares, each 2⅞" x 2⅞"	◺
A	2 squares, each 2½" x 2½"	
B	2 squares, each 2⅞" x 2⅞"	◺
C	10 squares, each 2½" x 2½"	
D	10 squares, each 2⅞" x 2⅞"	◺
E	3 squares, each 2⅞" x 2⅞"	◺
F	2 squares, each 2⅞" x 2⅞"	◺

◺ = cut squares once diagonally

1. Join the half-square triangles as shown to make pieced squares. Press the seam allowances in the direction indicated by the arrows.

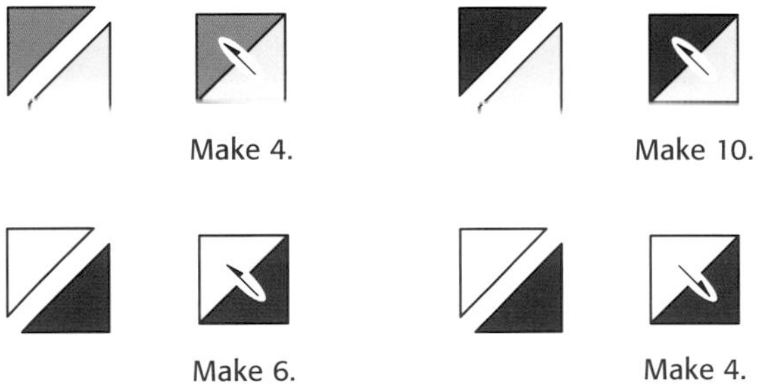

Make 4.   Make 10.

Make 6.   Make 4.

2. Join the pieced squares as shown to make units 1–5. Press the seam allowances in the direction indicated.

Unit 1
Make 2.

Unit 2
Make 2.

Unit 3
Make 2.

Unit 4
Make 1.

Unit 5
Make 2.

3. Arrange the units as shown into 3 horizontal rows of 3 units each. Stitch the units in each row together, pressing the seam allowances in the direction indicated. Stitch the rows together, pressing as shown.

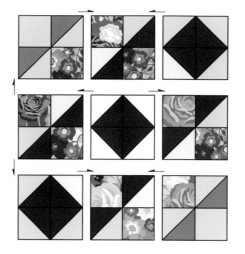

SQUARE AND STAR

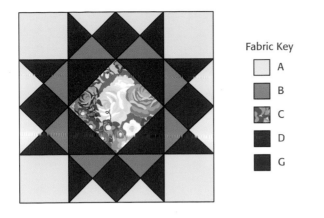

Fabric Key

A
B
C
D
G

Fabric	First Cut	Second Cut
A	4 squares, each 3½" x 3½"	
A	2 squares, each 4¼" x 4¼"	⊠
B	2 squares, each 4¼" x 4¼"	⊠
C	1 square, 4¾" x 4¾"	
D	2 squares, each 3⅞" x 3⅞"	◫
D	2 squares, each 4¼" x 4¼"	⊠
G	4 squares, each 2⅝" x 2⅝"	

◫ = cut squares once diagonally

⊠ = cut squares twice diagonally

1. Join one 3⅞" fabric D triangle to each side of the fabric C square to make the center unit. Press the seam allowances toward the fabric D triangles.

Center Unit
Make 1.

2. To make the side units, stitch one fabric A triangle and one fabric B triangle to opposite sides of each fabric G square as shown. Press the seam allowances toward the triangles. Stitch each of the remaining fabric A triangles to a fabric D quarter-square triangle. Stitch each of the remaining fabric D quarter-square triangles to a fabric B triangle. Press the seam allowances in the direction indicated by the arrows. Stitch the units together, pressing as shown. Make 4.

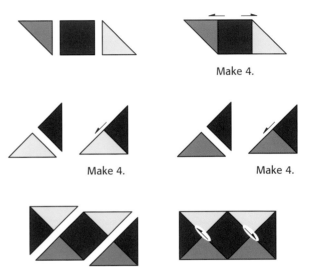

Make 4.

Make 4. Make 4.

Side Unit
Make 4.

3. Arrange the fabric A squares, the side units, and the center unit into rows as shown. Stitch the units in each row together, pressing the seam allowances as shown. Stitch the rows together, pressing as shown.

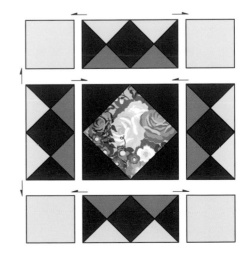

SPIDER'S DEN

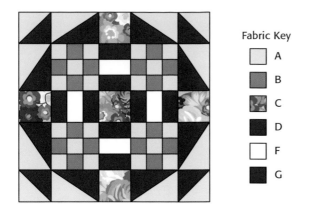

Fabric Key

A
B
C
D
F
G

Note: *Trace the pattern for the Spider's Den template (page 15) onto template plastic. Use the template to cut the required pieces from fabrics A and D.*

Fabric	First Cut	Second Cut
A	4 and 4 reversed of Spider's Den template	
A	2 squares, each 2⅞" x 2⅞"	◻
A	20 squares, each 1½" x 1½"	
B	16 squares, each 1½" x 1½"	
C	5 squares, each 2½" x 2½"	
D	4 and 4 reversed of Spider's Den template	
D	2 squares, each 2⅞" x 2⅞"	◻
F	4 rectangles, each 1½" x 2½"	
G	8 rectangles, each 1½" x 2½"	

◻ = cut squares once diagonally

1. Join fabric A and D template triangles to make units 1 and 2. Press the seam allowances toward the fabric D triangles. Make 4 of each unit shown.

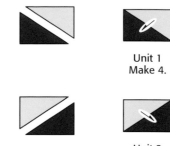

Unit 1
Make 4.

Unit 2
Make 4.

2. To make the nine-patch units, join five 1½" fabric A squares and four 1½" fabric B squares as shown. Press the seam allowances as shown. Make 4.

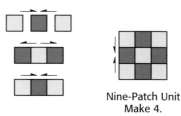

Nine-Patch Unit
Make 4.

3. To make unit 3, stitch a fabric G rectangle to each side of a fabric F rectangle. Press the seam allowances toward the fabric G rectangles. Make 4.

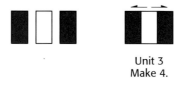

Unit 3
Make 4.

4. Join one 2⅞" fabric A triangle and one fabric D triangle to make a pieced square. Make 4.

Make 4.

5. Arrange the units, the pieced squares, and the fabric C squares into rows as shown. Stitch the units in each row together, pressing the seam allowances in the direction indicated. Stitch the rows together, pressing as shown.

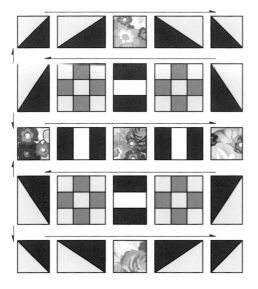

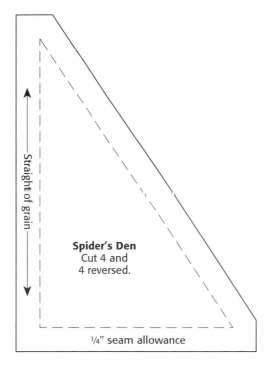

Straight of grain

Spider's Den
Cut 4 and
4 reversed.

¼" seam allowance

TWINKLING STAR

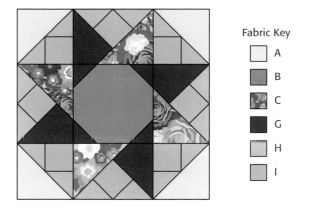

Fabric Key

A
B
C
G
H
I

Note: *Trace the Twinkling Star template pattern (page 16) onto template plastic. Use the template to cut the required pieces from fabric G.*

Fabric	First Cut	Second Cut
A	2 squares, each 4⅜" x 4⅜"	◻
B	1 square, 5½" x 5½"	
C	2 squares, each 4⅜" x 4⅜"	◻
G	4 of Twinkling Star template	
G	4 squares, each 2" x 2"	
H	4 squares, each 3¾" x 3¾"	⊠
I	8 squares, each 2¼" x 2¼"	

◻ = cut squares once diagonally

⊠ = cut squares twice diagonally

1. Stitch a fabric H quarter-square triangle to 2 adjacent sides of a fabric I square as shown. Press the seam allowances toward the triangles. Make 8.

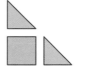

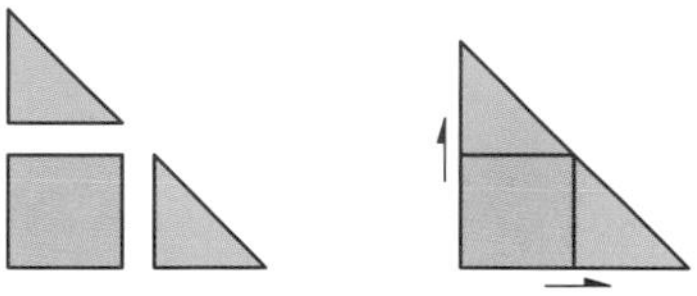

Make 8.

2. Stitch a pieced triangle from step 1 to each fabric A half-square triangle. Press the seam allowances toward the fabric A triangle. Make 4 of unit 1.

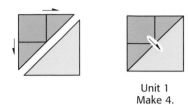

Unit 1
Make 4.

3. Stitch a Twinkling Star template piece and a fabric C half-square triangle to each of the remaining pieced triangles from step 1. Press the seam allowances in the direction indicated. Make 4 of unit 2.

Unit 2
Make 4.

4. Draw a diagonal line on the wrong sides of the 4 fabric G squares. Place a fabric G square over each corner of the fabric B square, right sides together. Align the corners, then sew on the diagonal lines. Trim ¼" from the stitching. Press toward fabric G to complete unit 3.

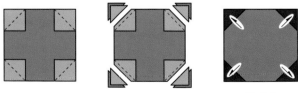

Unit 3
Make 1.

5. Arrange the units into 3 horizontal rows as shown. Stitch the units in each row together. Press the seam allowances in the direction indicated. Stitch the rows together, pressing as shown.

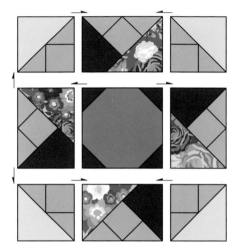

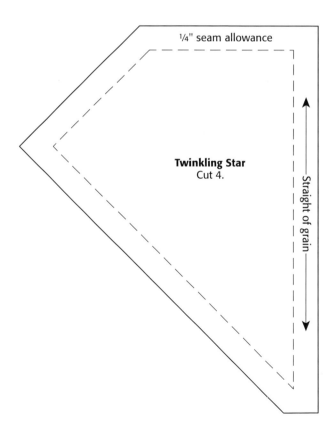

¼" seam allowance

Twinkling Star
Cut 4.

Straight of grain

STAR AND PINWHEEL

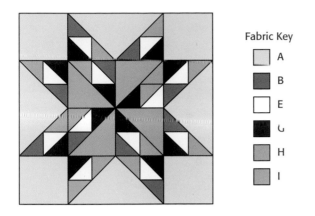

Fabric Key

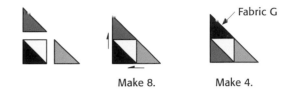

Fabric	First Cut	Second Cut
A	1 square, 7¼" x 7¼"	⊠
A	4 squares, each 3½" x 3½"	
B, G, H, and I	18 squares total, each 2⅜" x 2⅜", with at least 4 from fabric G	◰
E	6 squares, each 2⅜" x 2⅜"	◰
H	2 squares, each 3⅞" x 3⅞"	◰

◰ = cut squares once diagonally
⊠ = cut squares twice diagonally

1. Set aside 4 fabric G triangles; you'll use these in step 2. Then stitch each fabric E triangle to a 2⅜" fabric B, G, H, or I half-square triangle to make a pieced square. Make 12 total, pressing the seam allowance as shown.

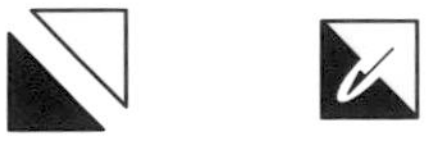

Make 12 total.

2. Stitch 2 of the remaining 2⅜" fabric B, G, H, or I half-square triangles to 2 adjacent sides of each pieced square to make a pieced triangle. Make at least 4 pieced triangles with a fabric G triangle on the same side of the pieced square. Set these 4 aside for the center square. Make 12 pieced triangles total.

Fabric G

Make 8.   Make 4.

3. Sew 1 pieced triangle to each short side of a fabric A triangle to make a pieced rectangle. Make 4.

Make 4.

4. Stitch a pieced triangle with the fabric G triangle on one side to each 3⅞" fabric H triangle. Stitch 4 pieced squares together as shown to make the center square.

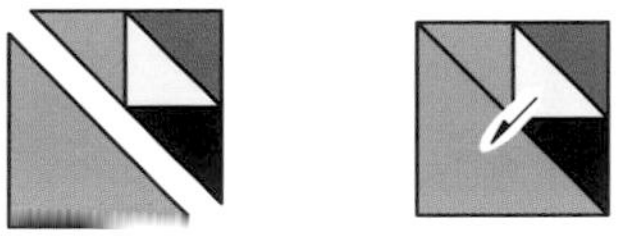

Make 4.

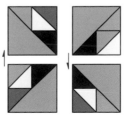

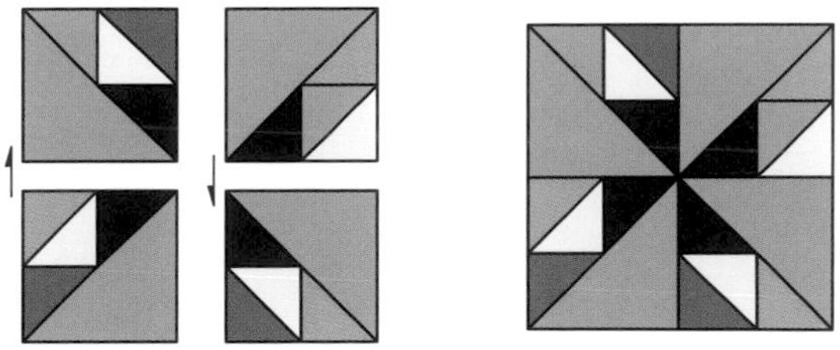

Center Square
Make 1.

5. Arrange the 4 fabric A squares and the pieced units into 3 horizontal rows as shown. Stitch the units in each row together, pressing the seam allowances in the direction indicated. Stitch the rows together, pressing as shown.

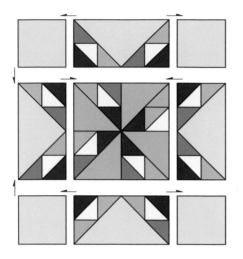

SALT LAKE CITY

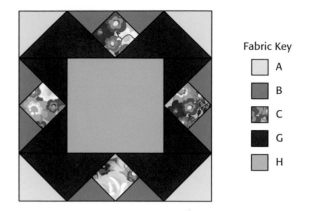

Fabric Key

▢	A
▨	B
▨	C
▰	G
▨	H

Fabric	First Cut	Second Cut
A	2 squares, each $3\frac{7}{8}$" x $3\frac{7}{8}$"	◹
B	2 squares, each $4\frac{1}{4}$" x $4\frac{1}{4}$"	⊠
C	4 squares, each $2\frac{5}{8}$" x $2\frac{5}{8}$"	
G	1 square, $7\frac{1}{4}$" x $7\frac{1}{4}$"	⊠
G	2 squares, each $3\frac{7}{8}$" x $3\frac{7}{8}$"	◹
H	1 square, $6\frac{1}{2}$" x $6\frac{1}{2}$"	

◹ = cut squares once diagonally

⊠ = cut squares twice diagonally

1. Stitch a fabric B triangle to 2 adjacent sides of a fabric C square as shown. Press the seam allowances toward the triangles. Make 4.

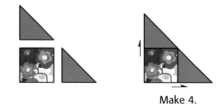

Make 4.

2. To make the top/bottom unit, stitch a fabric G quarter-square triangle to the side of a pieced triangle from step 1 as shown. Press the seam allowances toward the fabric G triangles. Stitch a fabric A triangle to the ends of the pieced unit

as shown. Press the seam allowances toward the fabric A triangles. Make 2.

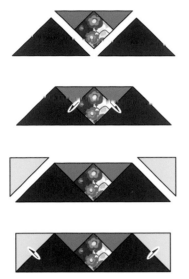

Top/Bottom Unit
Make 2.

3. Stitch 2 fabric G half-square triangles to each of the remaining pieced triangles from step 1. Press the seam allowances toward the fabric G triangles to make the side units. Make 2.

Side Unit
Make 2.

4. Stitch the side units to the sides of the fabric H square. Press the seam allowances toward the square. Stitch the top/bottom units to the top and bottom of the square. Press the seam allowances toward the square.

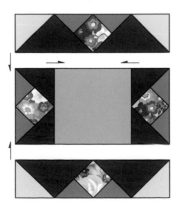

FERRIS WHEEL

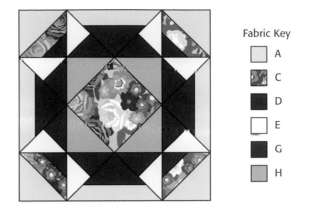

Fabric Key

▢	A
▨	C
◼	D
▢	E
◼	G
▨	H

Note: *Trace the patterns for templates 1 and 2 (page 20) onto template plastic. Use the templates to cut the required pieces from fabrics A and C.*

Fabric	First Cut	Second Cut
A	2 squares, each 3⅞" x 3⅞"	◺
A	4 of template 2	
C	1 square, 4¾" x 4¾"	
C	4 of template 1	
D	2 squares, each 4¼" x 4¼"	⊠
E	2 squares, each 4¼" x 4¼"	⊠
G	1 square, 5¼" x 5¼"	⊠
G	2 squares, each 2⅜" x 2⅜"	◺
H	2 squares, each 3⅞" x 3⅞"	◺

◺ = cut squares once diagonally

⊠ = cut squares twice diagonally

1. Join 1 fabric A triangle, 1 fabric C trapezoid (template 1), and 1 fabric G half-square triangle to make a pieced square. Press the seam allowances toward the fabric A triangle. Make 4.

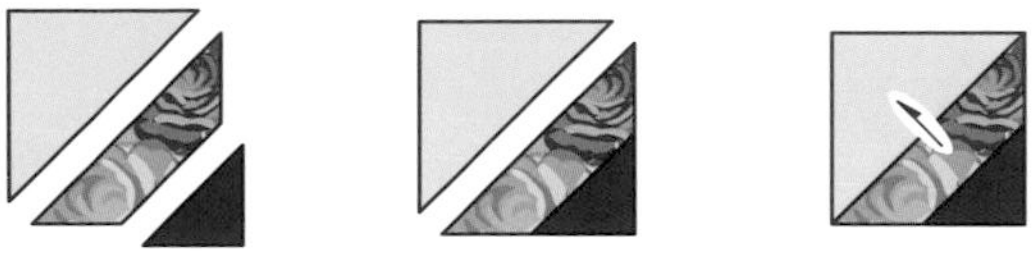

Make 4.

2. Join a fabric G quarter-square triangle to each fabric A trapezoid (template 2). Press the seam allowances toward the fabric G triangle. Make 4 fabric A/G pieced triangles. Join the fabric D and E triangles to make left-facing and right-facing triangle units as shown. Press the seam allowances toward the fabric D triangles. Make 4 of each. Stitch a left-facing and right-facing triangle unit to each fabric A/G pieced triangle as shown. Press the seams in the direction indicated. Make 4 pieced rectangles.

Make 4.

Make 4.   Make 4.

Make 4.

3. To make the center square, stitch the fabric H triangles to each side of the fabric C square. Press the seam allowances toward the triangles.

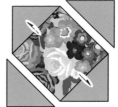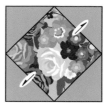

Center Square
Make 1.

4. Arrange the units into 3 horizontal rows as shown. Stitch the units in each row together. Press the seam allowances in the direction indicated. Join the rows, pressing as shown.

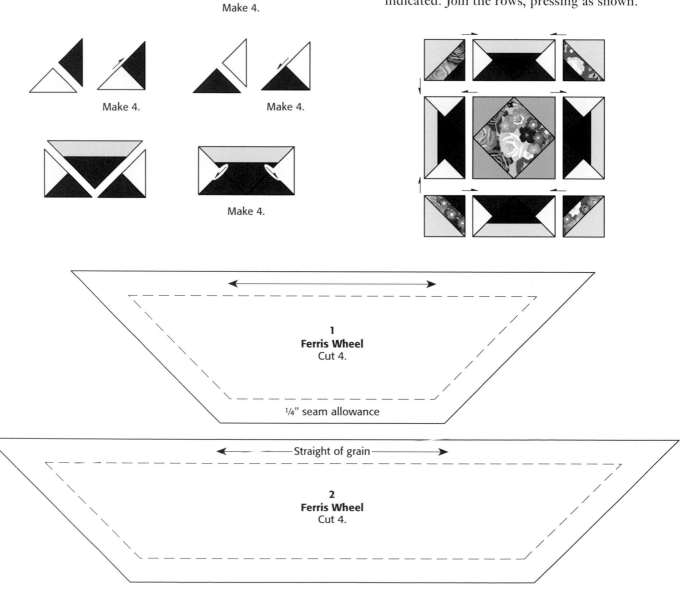

1
Ferris Wheel
Cut 4.

¼" seam allowance

←————— Straight of grain —————→

2
Ferris Wheel
Cut 4.

AUNT SUKEY'S CHOICE

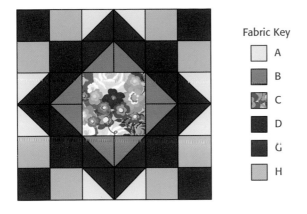

Fabric Key

☐	A
☐	B
☐	C
☐	D
☐	G
☐	H

Fabric	First Cut	Second Cut
A	4 squares, each 2⅞" x 2⅞"	◺
B	4 squares, each 2⅞" x 2⅞"	◺
C	1 square, 4½" x 4½"	
D	8 squares, each 2½" x 2½"	
G	8 squares, each 2⅞" x 2⅞"	◺
H	8 squares, each 2½" x 2½"	

◺ = cut squares once diagonally

1. Join 2 fabric D squares and 2 fabric H squares to make a four-patch square. Make 4.

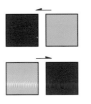

Four-Patch Unit
Make 4.

2. Stitch the fabric A, B, and G triangles together as shown to make pieced squares. Make 8 A/G squares and 8 B/G squares. Press the seam allowances in the direction indicated. Stitch 2 A/G squares and 2 B/G squares together as shown to make the pieced squares. Press the seam allowances in the direction indicated. Make 4.

Make 8.   Make 8.

Make 4.

3. Arrange the pieced units and the center square into 3 horizontal rows as shown. Stitch the units in each row together. Press the seam allowances in the direction indicated. Stitch the rows together, pressing as shown.

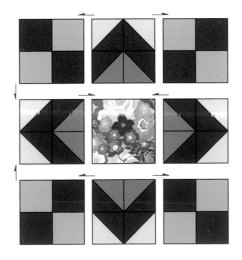

FRIENDSHIP STAR

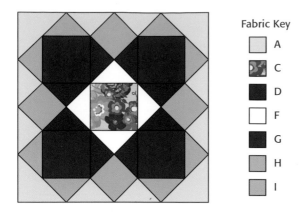

Fabric Key

A
C
D
F
G
H
I

Fabric	First Cut	Second Cut
A	2 squares, each 3⅞" x 3⅞"	◲
A	2 squares, each 4¼" x 4¼"	⊠
C	1 square, 3½" x 3½"	
D	2 squares, each 4¼" x 4¼"	⊠
F	1 square, 4¼" x 4¼"	⊠
G	4 squares, each 3½" x 3½"	
H	4 squares, each 2⅝" x 2⅝"	
I	2 squares, each 4¼" x 4¼"	⊠

◲ = cut squares once diagonally

⊠ = cut squares twice diagonally

1. Stitch 2 fabric D and 2 fabric I triangles to each fabric G square as shown to make a pieced square. Press the seam allowances toward the triangles. Make 4.

Make 4.

2. Stitch 4 fabric F triangles to the sides of the fabric C square to make the center square. Press the seam allowances toward the triangles.

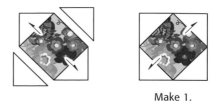

Make 1.

3. Stitch 2 fabric A quarter-square triangles to 2 adjacent sides of each fabric H square to make the pieced triangles. Make 4.

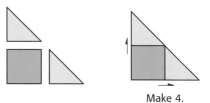

Make 4.

4. Arrange the pieced units and 2 fabric A half-square triangles in 3 diagonal rows as shown. Stitch the units in each row together. Press the seam allowances as shown. Stitch the rows together. Stitch the remaining 2 fabric A half-square triangles to the upper-left and lower-right corners.

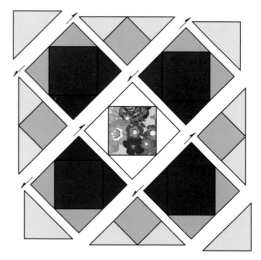

OLD FAVORITE

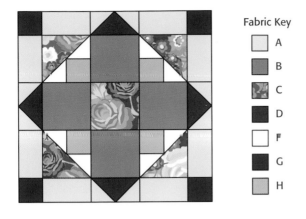

Fabric Key

- A
- B
- C
- D
- F
- G
- H

Fabric	First Cut	Second Cut
A	8 rectangles, each 2" x 3½"	
A	4 squares, each 2⅜" x 2⅜"	◺
B	4 squares, each 3½" x 3½"	
C	1 square, 3½" x 3½"	
C	2 squares, each 3⅞" x 3⅞"	◺
D	1 square, 4¼" x 4¼"	⊠
F	4 squares, each 2⅜" x 2⅜"	◺
G	4 squares, each 2" x 2"	
H	4 squares, each 2" x 2"	

◺ = cut squares once diagonally

⊠ = cut squares twice diagonally

1. Stitch 2 fabric F triangles to adjacent sides of each fabric H square. Press the seam allowances toward the triangles. Make 4 pieced triangles.

Stitch each pieced triangle to a fabric C triangle to make a pieced square. Press the seam allowances toward the fabric C triangle. Make 4.

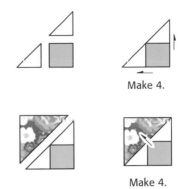

Make 4.

Make 4.

2. Join two fabric A triangles to the short sides of a fabric D triangle as shown. Press the seam allowances toward the fabric A triangles. Make 4 pieced triangles.

Unit 3
Make 4.

3. Arrange the pieced units, fabric G squares, fabric A rectangles, fabric B squares, and fabric C square into 5 horizontal rows as shown. Stitch the units in each row together. Press the seam allowances in the direction indicated. Stitch the rows together, pressing as shown.

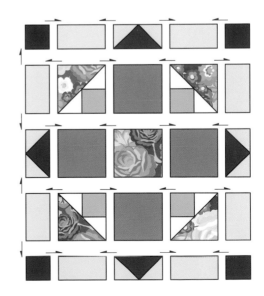

STAR-CROSSED CHRISTMAS

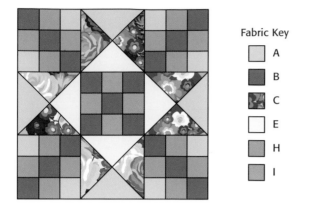

Fabric Key

	A
	B
	C
	E
	H
	I

Note: *Trace the pattern for the Star-Crossed Christmas template (page 25) onto template plastic. Use the template to cut the required pieces from fabrics A, B, H, and I.*

Fabric	First Cut	Second Cut
A	1 square, 5¼" x 5¼"	⊠
A	8 of Star-Crossed Christmas template	
B	17 of Star-Crossed Christmas template	
C	2 squares, each 5¼" x 5¼"	⊠
E	1 square, 5¼" x 5¼"	⊠
H	16 of Star-Crossed Christmas template	
I	4 of Star-Crossed Christmas template	

⊠ = cut squares twice diagonally

1. Stitch together 2 fabric A squares, 3 fabric B squares, and 4 fabric H squares to make a corner nine-patch unit. Press the seam allowances as shown. Make 4. Repeat with 5 fabric B squares and 4 fabric I squares to make the center nine-patch unit.

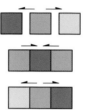

Corner
Nine-Patch Unit
Make 4.

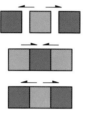

Center
Nine-Patch Unit
Make 1.

2. Join 1 fabric A triangle, 2 fabric C triangles, and 1 fabric E triangle to make a pieced square. Trim the square to measure 4½" x 4½". Make 4.

Make 4.

3. Arrange the units into 3 horizontal rows as shown. Stitch the units in each row together. Press the seam allowances in the direction indicated. Stitch the rows together, pressing as shown.

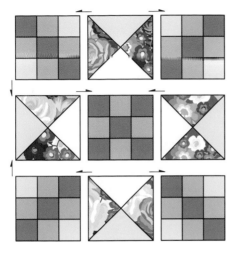

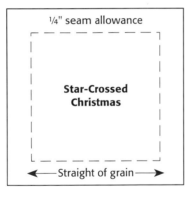

¼" seam allowance

Star-Crossed Christmas

←——— Straight of grain ———→

NORTHUMBERLAND STAR

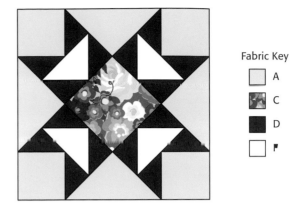

Fabric Key

▢	A
▨	C
▮	D
☐	F

Fabric	First Cut	Second Cut
A	4 squares, each 3½" x 3½"	
A	1 square, 7¼" x 7¼"	⊠
C	1 square, 4¾" x 4¾"	
D	8 squares, each 3" x 3"	◺
F	1 square, 5½" x 5½"	⊠

◺ = cut squares once diagonally

⊠ = cut squares twice diagonally

1. Stitch 2 fabric D triangles to 2 adjacent sides of a fabric A square to make unit 1. Press the seam allowances toward the triangles. Make 4.

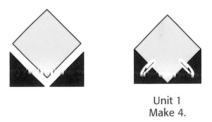

Unit 1
Make 4.

2. Sew 2 fabric D triangles to the short sides of a fabric F triangle to make unit 2. Press the seam allowances toward the fabric D triangles. Make 4.

Unit 2
Make 4.

3. Stitch each unit 1 to a unit 2 as shown to make unit 3. Press the seam allowances toward unit 2. Make 4.

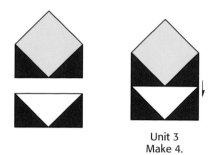

Unit 3
Make 4.

4. To make the side units, stitch 2 fabric A triangles to the sides of unit 3 as shown. Press the seam allowances toward the triangles. Make 2.

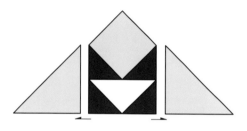

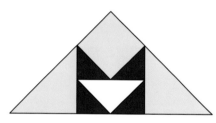

Side Unit
Make 2.

5. To make the center unit, sew a unit 3 to opposite sides of the fabric C square. Press the seam allowances toward the square.

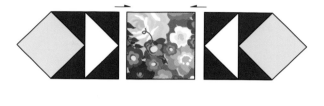

Center Unit
Make 1.

6. Stitch a side unit to the 2 long edges of the center unit, pressing as shown.

Dresden Fan Garden Quilt

By Carolann M. Palmer, 86" x 110"

This quilt is designed using 62 Double Fans, with 8 fan blades each, and 4 Dresden Fans, with 4 fan blades each. The quilt is large enough to cover a king-size bed; however, the design is easily adapted to a full/queen quilt—just see the box below.

Finished Quilt Size: 86" x 110"
Finished Block Size: 17" x 17"

Full/Queen Quilt

You can adjust the Dresden Fan Garden quilt to a full/queen quilt with a few easy changes. First, eliminate one row (three Dresden Fan Sampler blocks) from the center of the quilt. Then, from each of the two side borders, eliminate one 13¼" print triangle and one Double Fan trapezoid piece. The full/queen quilt measures 86" x 86".

MATERIALS

Yardage is based on 42"-wide fabric.

- 6½ yds. fabric for block and outer border backgrounds (fabric A)
- ½ yd. *each* of 7 or more assorted prints and solids for sampler blocks (fabrics B and D–I)
- 3½ yds. large-scale floral print for sampler blocks and outer border (fabric C)
- ¾ yd. *each* of 8 assorted prints and solids, in 8 gradations of one color, for fan blades
- ⅞ yd. for half-circles and quarter-circles
- 1¼ yds. for inner border and binding
- 7¾ yds. for backing
- 90" x 114" piece of batting

CUTTING

Cut all strips on the crosswise grain of the fabric. Measurements include ¼" seam allowances. Cut the pieces listed below first, and then use any remaining scraps in the 12 sampler blocks, if desired. Cutting directions for the sampler blocks are found on pages 11–26.

From the background fabric, cut:

- 3 strips, each 17½" x 42"; crosscut strips into 6 squares, each 17½" x 17½", for Double Fan blocks
- 3 strips, each 25¼" x 42"; crosscut strips into 3 squares, each 25¼" x 25¼". Cut squares twice diagonally to yield 12 setting triangles (you will use 10 triangles and have 2 left over).
- 2 squares, each 13" x 13"; cut each square once diagonally to yield 4 corner triangles.
- 7 strips, each 6½" x 42"; make a trapezoid template from paper, using the Outer Border Trapezoid diagram on page 31 and sizing as instructed. Using the template, cut 14 trapezoids from strips for outer border.
- 4 squares, each 6½" x 6½", for outer border corners

From the large-scale floral print, cut:

- 6 strips, each 10" x 42"; crosscut strips into 24 squares, each 10" x 10". Cut squares once diagonally to yield 48 triangles for sampler blocks.
- 1 strip, 13¼" x 42"; crosscut strip into 3 squares, each 13¼" x 13¼". Cut squares twice diagonally to yield 12 triangles for outer border. (You'll use 10 triangles and have 2 left over.)
- 1 strip, 6⅞" x 42"; crosscut strip into 4 squares, each 6⅞" x 6⅞". Cut squares once diagonally to yield 8 triangles for outer border corners.

From the inner border, outer border, and binding fabric, cut:

- 10 strips, each 1½" x 42", for inner border. From 1 of the strips, cut 4 pieces, each 1½" x 6½"; you will use these 4 pieces in the outer border.
- 10 strips, each 2½" x 42", for binding

BLOCK ASSEMBLY

1. Make 1 each of the 12 blocks on pages 11–26.
2. Stitch one 10" floral triangle to each side of each pieced block as shown. Trim the blocks to measure 17½" x 17½".

Unit A
Make 12 total.

3. Make templates for the fan blade (template 3), half-circle (template 4), and quarter-circle (template 5) using the patterns on page 31. Referring to "Freezer-Paper Appliqué," steps 1–3 on pages 5–6, cut 496 fan blades from the assorted prints for fan blades. From the

half- and quarter-circle fabric, cut 62 half-circles and 4 quarter-circles.

4. Refer to "Piecing the Dresden Units" on page 7 to piece 62 Double Fan units and 4 Dresden Fan units.

5. Referring to "Traditional Appliqué Stitch" on page 7, center a Double Fan unit on each side of the 17½" x 17½" background squares; appliqué the fan blades in place. Make 6 Double Fan blocks. Appliqué a Double Fan unit to each of 14 outer-border trapezoids, centering the appliqué on the 12½" edge of the trapezoid. Also appliqué a Double Fan unit to the long edge of each corner triangle and both short edges of each setting triangle. Appliqué a Dresden Fan unit to each outer-border corner square. Appliqué the half-circles to the Double Fan units and the quarter-circles to the Dresden Fan units. Cut away the background fabric behind each unit and remove the freezer-paper templates.

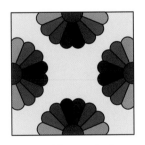

Double Fan Block
Make 6.

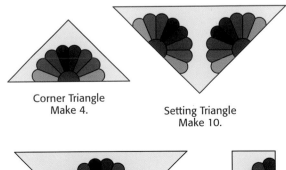

Corner Triangle
Make 4.

Setting Triangle
Make 10.

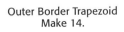

Outer Border Trapezoid
Make 14.

Outer Border
Corner Square
Make 4.

QUILT ASSEMBLY AND FINISHING

1. Alternately arrange the sampler blocks and Double Fan blocks in 6 diagonal rows as shown. Sew the blocks in each row together, stitching corner or setting triangles to the ends of each row as shown. Join the rows. Stitch a corner triangle to the remaining corners. Press the seam allow-ances in opposite directions from row to row.

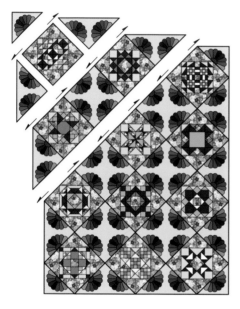

2. Stitch the nine 1½" x 42" inner border strips together to make 1 long strip.

3. Join the trapezoids with Double Fans, the 13¼" print triangles, 6⅞" print triangles, 1½" x 6½" outer border pieces, and Dresden Fan squares into outer border strips.

Side Border
Make 2.

Top and Bottom Border
Make 2.

4. From the long inner border strip sewn in step 2, cut 2 segments, each 1½" x 96½". Stitch 1 inner border segment to each side outer border strip as shown. From the remaining inner border strip, cut 2 segments, each 1½" x 86½". Stitch 1 segment to each top and bottom outer border strip as shown.

5. Mark the center of the side edges of the quilt and the center of the side pieced border strips. Pin the side pieced border strips to the sides of the quilt top, matching the centers and ends and easing as necessary. Sew the pieced border strips in place. Press the seams toward the pieced border strips. Repeat with the top and bottom pieced border strips.

6. Layer the quilt top with batting and backing; baste. Quilt as desired.

7. Bind the edges and add a label.

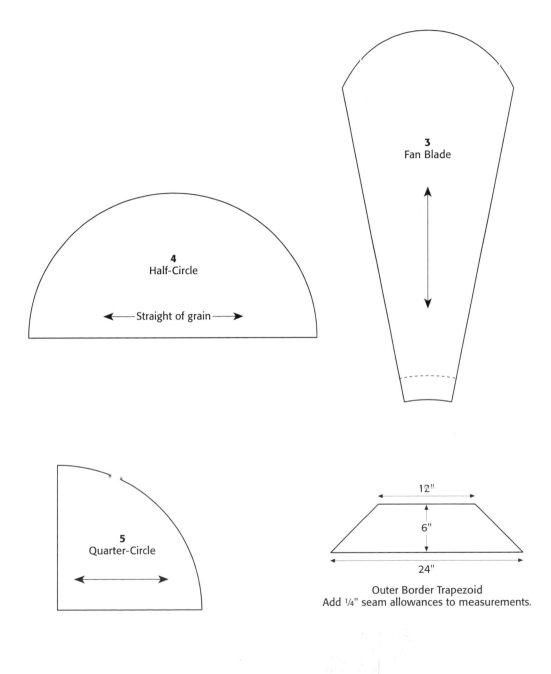

3
Fan Blade

4
Half-Circle

← Straight of grain →

5
Quarter-Circle

12"

6"

24"

Outer Border Trapezoid
Add ¼" seam allowances to measurements.

European Square-Pillow Shams

By Cleo Nollette, 32" x 32".

These European square-pillow shams are designed to fit 26" pillow forms. The center of the sham features a Northumberland Star Sampler block, accented with Double Fans at each corner. You may substitute any of the 12" blocks from pages 11–26 for the center.

Finished Pillow-Sham Size: 32" x 32"
Finished Block Size: 24" x 24"

MATERIALS (FOR 1 PILLOW SHAM)

Yardage is based on 42"-wide fabric.

- 5/8 yd. for background and inner border
- 1/2 yd. large-scale floral print for sampler block
- 1/4 yd. *total* assorted scraps of 3 or more fabrics for sampler block
- 1/2 yd. for flange
- 3/8 yd. *total* scraps of 8 or more assorted prints and solids, in 8 gradations of one color, for fan blades
- 1/8 yd. solid for half-circles
- 1 yd. fabric for pillow-sham top backing
- 1 yd. fabric for pillow-sham back
- 35" x 35" square of batting
- 26" x 26" pillow form

CUTTING

Cut all strips on the crosswise grain of the fabric. Measurements include 1/4" seam allowances, unless otherwise noted. Make one sampler block of your choice or make the Northumberland Star block shown here.

Cut the pieces listed below first, and then use any remaining scraps in the sampler block, if desired. Cutting directions for the 12" sampler blocks are found on pages 11–26.

From the background fabric, cut:

- 2 squares, each 13" x 13"; cut squares once diagonally to make 4 triangles for sampler block
- 2 strips, each 1½" x 24½", for side borders

- 2 strips, each 1½" x 26½", for top and bottom borders

From the large-scale floral print fabric, cut:

- 2 squares, each 10" x 10"; cut squares once diagonally to make 4 triangles for sampler block

From the flange fabric, cut:

- 2 strips, each 3½" x 26½", for side flanges
- 2 strips, each 3½" x 32½", for top and bottom flanges

From the backing fabric, cut:

- 1 square, 35" x 35"

From the pillow-sham back fabric, cut:

- 2 rectangles, each 21" x 32½"

DIRECTIONS

1. Make one 12" (finished) sampler block of your choice from pages 11–26.
2. Stitch one 10" floral triangle to each side of the pieced block as shown. Trim the square to measure 17½" x 17½".

Make 1.

33

3. Make templates for the fan blade (template 3) and half-circle (template 4) using the patterns on page 31. Referring to "Freezer-Paper Appliqué," steps 1–3 on pages 5–6, cut 32 fan blades from the assorted prints and solids for fan blades. From the solid fabric for half-circles, cut 4 half-circles.

4. Refer to "Piecing the Dresden Units" on page 7 to piece 4 Double Fan units. Center 1 unit on the long bias edge of each background triangle. Refer to "Traditional Appliqué Stitch" on page 7 to appliqué the units in place; then appliqué the half-circles in place. Cut away the background fabric behind each unit and remove the freezer-paper templates.

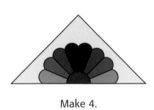

Make 4.

5. Stitch the appliquéd background triangles to each side of the pieced block from step 2. The block should measure 24½" x 24½".

Make 1.

6. Stitch the side border strips to the sides of the pillow top. Stitch the top and bottom border strips to the top and bottom edges. Press the seams toward the border strips. Join the side flange strips to the sides of the pillow top. Join the top and bottom flange strips to the top and bottom edges. Press the seams toward the flange strips.

7. Layer the pillow top with batting and backing; baste. Quilt as desired.

8. Press under 1" twice on one 32½" edge of each pillow-sham back piece to make double-fold hems. Stitch close to the first fold of each piece to secure.

9. Place the pillow-sham back pieces on the quilted sham front, right sides together, overlapping the hemmed edges of the back pieces by 5½"; pin.

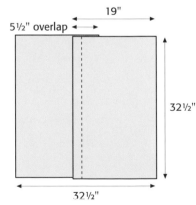

10. Stitch ½" from the raw edges. Trim the seam allowances. Turn right side out and press. Stitch in the ditch between the flange and inner border, through all layers. Insert the pillow form.

Dresden Plate Round Pillow

By Cleo Nollette, 14" diameter

This round toss pillow features a Dresden Plate in the middle. It is finished with a boxing strip and contrasting covered cording. Stuff the pillow cover with a 14" round pillow form, or use a square pillow form and simply push the corners in.

MATERIALS

Yardage is based on 42"-wide fabric.

- 1½ yds. light print for background of Dresden Plate, boxing strip, and pillow back
- ¼ yd. *total* scraps of 8 or more assorted prints and solids, in 8 gradations of one color, for fan blades
- ½ yd. dark solid for Dresden Plate circle and covered cording
- ½ yd. fabric for pillow-top backing
- 17" x 17" square of batting
- 14"-round pillow form
- 3 yds. ³⁄₁₆"-diameter cotton cord

CUTTING

Cut all strips on the crosswise grain of the fabric, unless otherwise noted. Measurements include ½" seam allowances, unless otherwise noted.

From the light print, cut:

- 1 strip, 3" x 45", for boxing strip. Cut this strip on the lengthwise grain.
- 1 circle, 15" in diameter, for pillow front (refer to step 1 below)
- 2 squares, each 17" x 17", for pillow back

From the backing fabric, cut:

- 1 square, 17" x 17"

DIRECTIONS

1. Trace or photocopy the pattern for the round pillow (page 37) onto paper 4 times. Cut out the patterns and tape the 4 pieces together, aligning the corners in the center to make a full circle measuring 15" in diameter. Using the pattern, cut 1 pillow-front piece from light print fabric. Set aside.

2. Make templates for the fan blade (template 5) and circle (template 6) using the patterns on pages 31 and 36. Referring to "Freezer-Paper Appliqué," steps 1–3 on pages 5–6, cut 16 fan blades from the assorted prints and solids for fan blades. From the dark solid, cut 1 circle.

3. Refer to "Piecing the Dresden Units" on page 7 to piece 1 Dresden Plate unit. Center the unit on the 15" light-print circle. Referring to "Traditional Appliqué Stitch" on page 7, appliqué the Dresden Plate in place; then

appliqué the circle to the Dresden Plate center. Cut away the background fabric behind the appliqué and remove the freezer-paper templates.

4. Press under ¼" on one side of each 17" light-print square for the pillow back, and then press under 4¾" on the same edge. Stitch close to the second fold.

5. With right sides up, overlap the hemmed edges of the pillow-back pieces by 4¾". Pin the hemmed edges together. Center and pin the pillow pattern onto the pillow-back pieces. Cut around the edge of the pattern to trim the pillow-back pieces to size. Remove the pattern. Baste the pillow-back pieces together, a scant ½" from the raw edges, along the width of the overlapped hems. Remove the pins.

6. Layer the pillow front with the batting and backing; baste. Quilt as desired. Trim the edges of the batting and backing even with the pillow front.

7. Referring to "Covered Cording" on page 8, make 3 yards of covered cording. Attach the cording to the raw edges of the pillow front and back, following steps 1–3 of "Covered Cording."

8. With right sides together, stitch the short ends of the boxing strip together. Press the seam allowances open. Quarter-mark the edges of the boxing strip and the outer edges of the pillow

front and back with pins. Pin the boxing strip to the pillow front, right sides together, matching the pin marks.

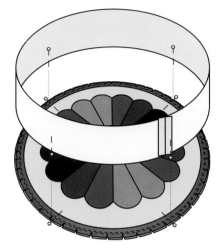

9. With the pillow front on top, stitch as close as possible to the cording.

10. Pin the pillow back to the boxing strip, right sides together, matching the pin marks. With the pillow-back pieces on top, stitch as close as possible to the cording. Trim and clip the seam allowances. Turn right side out and insert the pillow form.

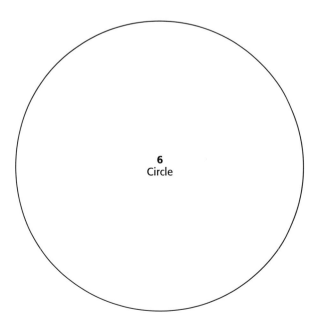

6
Circle

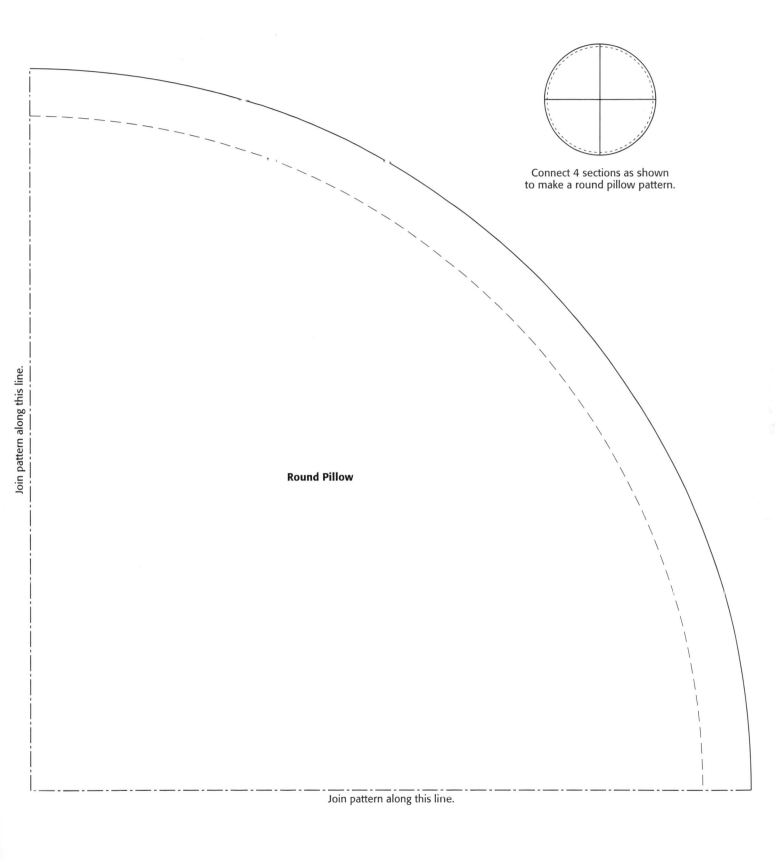

Connect 4 sections as shown
to make a round pillow pattern.

Join pattern along this line.

Round Pillow

Join pattern along this line.

Ruffle-Edged Pillowcases

By Cleo Nollette, 20" x 29¾" for standard-size pillowcases (20" x 39¾" for king-size pillowcases)

Make a pair of special pillowcases to complement the Dresden Fan Garden quilt. These are designed with adequate length to prevent the pillow form from showing at the open edge of the case. Fabric yardage and directions are given for standard-size pillowcases, and the necessary information for king-size pillowcases appears in parentheses.

MATERIALS (FOR 2 PILLOWCASES)

Yardage is based on 42"-wide fabric. The first yardage listed is for standard-size pillowcases; yardage for king-size pillowcases is given in parentheses.

- 1¾ yds. (2⅜ yds.) light print for pillowcases
- ⅞ yd. dark print for ruffle
- ½ yd. fabric for covered cording
- 2½ yds. ³⁄₁₆"-diameter cotton cord

CUTTING

Cut all strips on the crosswise grain of the fabric. Measurements include seam and hem allowances as noted in the directions.

From the light print, cut:
- 2 rectangles, each 27" x 41½" (37" x 41½"), for pillowcases

From the dark print, cut:
- 4 strips, each 6" x 42", for ruffle

DIRECTIONS

1. Fold each light print rectangle in half, wrong sides together, to make a 27" x 20½" (37" x 20½") rectangle. Stitch a scant ¼" from the raw edges along one short end and on the long raw edges. Trim the corner where the seams meet.

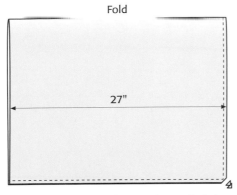

Fold

27"

Fold fabric wrong sides together and stitch.

2. Referring to "Covered Cording" on page 8, make 2½ yards of covered cording. Attach the cording to the raw edge of the pillowcase openings, following steps 1–3 of "Covered Cording."

3. Join 2 ruffle pieces, right sides together, along the short ends to make a continuous circle of fabric. Press the seam allowances open and finish with zigzag stitching, or press the seam allowances to one side and finish with a serged edge. Press under ¼" on one long edge, and then press under 1¾" on the same edge. Stitch close to the second fold to make a 1¾" hem. Repeat with the remaining 2 ruffle strips.

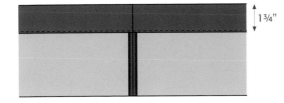

1¾"

4. Stitch 2 rows of gathering stitches along the edge opposite the ruffle hems, stitching ¼" and ⅜" from the raw edges. Quarter-mark the raw edge of the ruffles and the edge of the pillowcases with pins. Pull up the gathering threads and distribute the gathers evenly. Matching the pin marks, pin the ruffle to the pillowcase, right sides together, with the corded edge of the pillowcase on top.

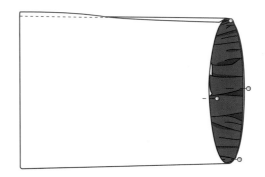

5. Stitch along the edge of the cording, over previous stitches or just inside the previous stitching line. Finish the raw edges with zigzag or serger stitching.

6. Press the seam allowances toward the inside of the pillowcases. From the right side, topstitch ¼" from the edge of the covered cording, through all layers, securing the seam allowances in place.

Double-Ruffle Bed Skirt

By Cleo Nollette

For a finished look on the bed, make a double-ruffle bed skirt to coordinate with the Dresden Fan Garden quilt. This bed skirt has split corners to allow for bedposts if necessary. Standard bed skirts measure 14" from the top of the box spring to just above the floor. This skirt has a top ruffle with a 10" drop and a bottom ruffle with a 14" drop. If your bed sits higher off the ground, adjust the length of the ruffle pieces. The skirt is attached to a platform that lies between the box spring and mattress. Purchase a flat sheet to use for the platform. Directions are given for full, queen, and king bed skirts.

Standard Mattress Sizes

Full	54" x 75"
Queen	60" x 80"
King	76" x 80"

MATERIALS

Yardage is based on 42"-wide fabric. The first yardage listed is for a full-size bed; queen and king sizes are given in parentheses.

- 4¾ yds. (5 yds., 5⅜ yds.) light print for top ruffle
- 6 yds. (6½ yds., 7 yds.) dark print for bottom ruffle
- Full-size (queen, king) flat sheet for bed-ruffle platform
- 6 yds. (6½ yds., 7 yds.) of thin, strong cord

CUTTING

Cut all strips on the crosswise grain of the fabric. Measurements include seam and hem allowances as noted in the directions.

From the light print, cut:

- 13 strips (14, 15), each 12½" x 42", for top ruffle

From the dark print, cut:

- 13 strips (14, 15), each 16½" x 42", for bottom ruffle

DIRECTIONS

1. Join the light print strips, right sides together, on the short ends, using ½" seam allowances. Press the seams open and finish with zigzag stitching, or press them to one side and finish with a serged edge.

2. Referring to the chart "Standard Mattress Sizes" (page 40), multiply the short mattress dimension by 2½, and cut 1 piece this length from the light print strip for the end of the bed. Multiply the long mattress dimension by 2½, and cut 2 pieces this length from the light print strip for the sides of the bed.

3. Press under ¼" on the ends of the strips, then press under 1" again. Stitch close to the first fold to hem the sides of the bed-skirt sections. Press under ¼" on one long edge of each section. Press under ¼" on the same side. Stitch close to the first fold. Repeat for each section. The bed-skirt sections should measure 10½" deep.

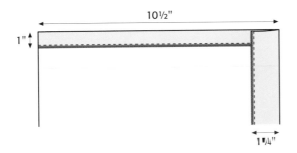

4. Repeat steps 1–3 with the dark print strips to make 3 bed-skirt sections, each 14½" deep.

5. Pin a light bed-skirt section onto a dark bed-skirt section, right sides up, matching the raw edges. To gather the sections, set your machine for a wide zigzag stitch and zigzag over a piece of thin, strong cord, ⅜" from the raw edges, being careful not to catch the cord in the stitching. Repeat with the remaining 2 sections.

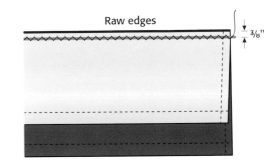

6. Referring to the chart "Standard Mattress Sizes" on page 40, trim the flat sheet to measure ½" longer and 1" wider than your mattress, using one hemmed edge of the sheet at the head of the bed.

7. Divide each unhemmed edge of the flat sheet into quarters and pin-mark. Quarter-mark the raw edges of the 3 bed-skirt sections. Pull on the cord to gather the bed-skirt sections to fit. Pin the end bed-skirt section to the short edge of the sheet, placing the light strip next to the flat sheet's right side and matching the pin marks. Adjust the gathers as necessary. Stitch ½" from the raw edges. Repeat on the 2 long sides of the sheet with the remaining bed-skirt sections.

Spring Flowers Wall Hanging

By Cleo Nollette, 36" x 36"

Decorate a wall in your kitchen or sunroom with this Dresden Fan wall hanging. You may substitute any of the 12" blocks from pages 11–26 for the center. If you choose to use the Twinkling Star block shown here, note that five fabrics used in the block are placed differently from those shown in the block-making section.

Finished Wall Hanging Size: 36" x 36"
Finished Block Size: 24" x 24"

MATERIALS

Yardage is based on 42"-wide fabric.

- ⅝ yd. light print for background and inner border
- 1 yd. dark floral print for outer block triangles and outer border
- ⅜ yd. dark solid for half-circles and binding
- ¼ yd. *total* assorted scraps of 5 or more fabrics for sampler block
- ⅜ yd. *total* scraps of 8 assorted prints and solids, in 8 gradations of one color, for fan blades
- 1¼ yds. fabric for backing
- 40" x 40" square of batting

CUTTING

Cut all strips on the crosswise grain of the fabric. Measurements include ¼" seam allowances. Make one sampler block of your choice or make the Twinkling Star block shown here. Cutting directions for the 12" sampler blocks are found on pages 11–26.

From the background fabric, cut:

- 2 squares, each 13" x 13"; cut the squares once diagonally to make 4 triangles for sampler block
- 2 strips, each 1½" x 24½", for inner side borders
- 2 strips, each 1½" x 26½", for inner top and bottom borders

From the medium floral print, cut:

- 2 squares, each 10" x 10"; cut the squares once diagonally to make 4 triangles for sampler block
- 2 strips, each 5¼" x 26½", for outer side borders
- 2 strips, each 5¼" x 36", for outer top and bottom borders

From the medium solid, cut:

- 4 strips, each 2½" x 42", for binding

DIRECTIONS

1. Make one 12" (finished) sampler block of your choice from pages 11–26.
2. Join one 10" floral triangle to each side of the pieced block as shown. Trim the square to measure 17½" x 17½".

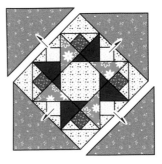

3. Make templates for the fan blade (template 3) and half-circle (template 4) using the patterns on page 31. Referring to "Freezer-Paper Appliqué," steps 1–3 on pages 5–6, cut 32 fan blades from the assorted prints and solids for fan blades. From the dark solid fabric, cut 4 half-circles.

4. Refer to "Piecing the Dresden Units" on page 7 to piece 4 Double Fan units. Center each unit on the long edge of each of the 4 background triangles. Refer to "Traditional Appliqué Stitch" on page 7 to appliqué the units in place; then appliqué the half-circles in place. Cut away the background fabric behind each unit and remove the freezer-paper templates.

Make 4.

5. Stitch the appliquéd triangles to each side of the square from step 2. The block should measure 24½" x 24½".

6. Stitch the inner side border strips to the sides of the block. Stitch the inner top and bottom border strips to the top and bottom edges. Press the seams toward the border strips. Stitch the outer side border strips to the sides of the quilt top. Stitch the outer top and bottom border strips to the top and bottom edges of the quilt top. Press the seams toward the outer border strips.

7. Layer the wall hanging top with batting and backing; baste. Quilt as desired.
8. Bind the edges and add a label.

Northumberland Star
Table Runner

By Bridget Haugh, 18" x 58"

Combine two Double Fan blocks with three sampler blocks to make a table runner for a kitchen or dining room. You can select one 12" block and repeat it three times, or you can use three different 12" blocks. Choose from any of the blocks on pages 11–26. The Northumberland Star block was used here. This versatile design can also be used to make a vertical wall hanging or a dresser scarf.

MATERIALS

Yardage is based on 42"-wide fabric.

- ¼ yd. white-on-white print for background
- 2 yds. for inner border, sashing, binding, and backing
- ⅜ yd. for outer border
- ½ yd. *total* scraps of 3 or more assorted prints for sampler blocks
- ⅜ yd. *total* scraps of 4 or more assorted prints for fan blades
- ⅛ yd. or scraps for half-circles
- 22" x 62" rectangle of batting

CUTTING

Cut all strips on the crosswise grain of the fabric, unless otherwise noted. Measurements include ¼" seam allowances. Cut the pieces listed below first, and then use any remaining scraps in the sampler blocks, if desired. Cutting directions for the 12" sampler blocks are found on pages 11–26.

From the white-on-white print, cut:

- 2 rectangles, each 6½" x 12½", for background of Double Fans blocks

From the inner border, sashing, binding, and backing fabric, cut on the lengthwise grain:

- 1 rectangle, 22" x 62", for backing
- 6 strips, each 1½" x 12½", for sashing and inner top and bottom borders
- 2 strips, each 1½" x 54½", for inner side border
- 3 strips, each 2½" x 62", for binding

From the outer border fabric, cut:

- 5 strips, each 2½" x 42"

DIRECTIONS

1. Make three sampler blocks of your choice from pages 11–26.
2. Make templates for the fan blade (template 3) and half-circle (template 4) using the patterns on page 31. Referring to "Freezer-Paper Appliqué," steps 1–3 on pages 5–6, cut 16 fan blades from the assorted prints for fan blades. From the half-circle fabric, cut 2 half-circles.
3. Refer to "Piecing the Dresden Units" on page 7 to piece 2 Double Fan units. Center each unit on the long edge of each background rectangle. Refer to "Traditional Appliqué Stitch" on page 7 to appliqué the units in place; then appliqué the half-circles in place. Cut away the background fabric behind each unit and remove the freezer-paper templates.

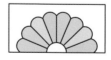

4. Join the three sampler blocks and the 2 Double Fan blocks, adding the sashing strips between them.

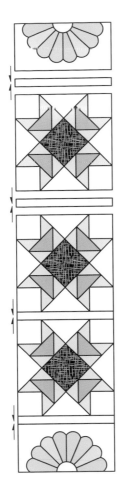

border strips. Stitch the outer side border strips to the quilt top sides. Press the seam allowances toward the outer border strips. Stitch the outer top and bottom border strips to the quilt top and bottom edges. Press the seam allowances toward the outer border strips.

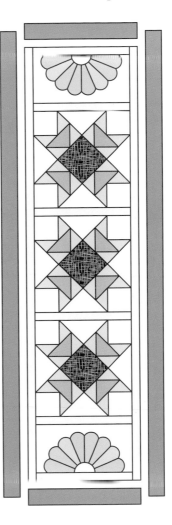

5. Add the 1½" x 12½" inner top and bottom border strips to the top and bottom edges. Press the seam allowances toward the border strips. Stitch the inner side border strips to the sides. Press the seam allowances toward the border strips.

6. Stitch the outer border strips together end to end to make 1 long strip. From the strip, cut 2 segments, each 2½" x 54½", for the outer side border strips, and 2 segments, each 2½" x 18½", for the outer top and bottom

7. Layer the quilt top with batting and backing; baste. Quilt as desired.

8. Bind the edges and add a label.

About the Author

Carolann M. Palmer is an enthusiastic quilting teacher, designer, and author. She has written four books and one pattern for That Patchwork Place and has self-published one other book. She is active in her local quilt guild and in two smaller groups. In addition to teaching in the Seattle area, she has taught quilting in Canada, Austria, Japan, and Australia.

Carolann has been actively quilting for forty-five years, first learning the art from her mother. She loves making baby quilts and has made more than three hundred for family and friends. Her inspiration for quilt designs comes from everything she sees, from nature to tiles, sidewalks, and other everyday objects. She enjoys introducing students to the art of quilting, and she believes making beautiful quilts is fun, and that each one becomes a wonderful learning experience.

When she's not teaching, Carolann enjoys spending time at her cabin in the woods.